WHY MEN & WOMEN MUST HEAL IN ORDER TO FIND TRUE LOVE

How to Heal a Broken Heart.

By

Dr Morgan O. Kate

Dr Morgan O. Kate

TABLE OF CONTENT

Introduction..

ChapterOne..

If You Want To Find Love, You Have To Heal Yourself First

ChapterTwo..

How to Heal a Broken Heart When a Relationship Ends

ChapterThree..

How to Find Real, Lasting Love without Looking for It

Chapter Four..

The Importance of Healing After a Breakup

What should you NOT do after a breakup?

ChapterFive..

What are the stages of healing after a breakup?

Chapter Six..

Steps for How to Move On

INTRODUCTION

Mending a broken heart takes self-compassion. It can't be rushed, and it might take some time, but healing is possible.

Breakups usually aren't easy, whether your ex-partner ended the relationship or you did. Reminiscing about the happy moments during your time together can make the breakup hard to get past.

Whatever you're feeling right now is normal, though — whether that's loneliness, humiliation, rejection, disconnection, disappointment, or even relief.

Love has unbelievable healing powers, literally. Believe it or not, positive relationships and love can make flesh wounds heal much faster. To prove this point, scientists at the Ohio State University Medical Centre studied the blister wounds of married couples. They found that these wounds healed much faster in partners who had a happy married life as compared to those who shared a hostile relationship with his or her spouse.

To help you better navigate the healing process, we'll explain why heartbreak is happening in the first place. We'll also review some tips on how to move past it.

What causes heartbreak when a relationship ends?

Morgan O. Kate, a psychotherapist based in Canada, says that at the start of a relationship, our thoughts tend to be happy and uplifting. "We may have felt good about ourselves — thoughts about the time our ex commented that we were beautiful or handsome or how much they loved us," she says.

However, when the relationship ends, your thoughts may be mixed. "We have the positive messages that were given by our ex, combined with perhaps our own judgmental thoughts that we are not good enough or thoughts that things never work out for us," explains Bottari.

Thoughts affect feelings, and feelings affect actions, she says. When you're feeling down, you may engage in behaviours you typically don't. For example, you may skip showering or avoid getting together with friends and family. "We may now feel more alone than ever," Bottari says.

Thoughts affect feelings, and feelings affect actions, she says. When you're feeling down, you may engage in behaviours you typically don't. For example, you may skip showering or avoid getting together with friends and family. "We may now feel more alone than ever.

Gina Moffa, LCSW, a psychotherapist based in New York City, adds that the details and circumstances of a breakup determine how you feel.

"If you feel you're leaving someone in a painful place after you end it, you may be ridden with guilt and sadness. If you're the one who's been broken up with, you may be in a state of shock and go through different phases of grief, including anger, bargaining, depression, and anxiety.

CHAPTER ONE

If You Want To Find Love, You Have To Heal Yourself First

Soulmates only come when you've done the inner work.

Love. What is the first thing that comes to your mind when you read that word? Is it joy and intimacy? Is it pain and discomfort? Is it vulnerability?

There's a reason why I'm asking this question. What you perceive love to be, is exactly what you'll experience in your relationships.

If you see relationships as something complicated that takes all your freedom away, then that's the type of relationships you'll attract. If you believe that love is painful and that it inevitably leads to suffering, guess what? You'll always end up in relationships that make you suffer.

If, on the contrary, you see love as this amazing feeling that lights you up, you'll invite into your life people and situations that will prove to you that love is, indeed, fascinating.

What you focus on, grows. It's as simple as that.

We've all gone through relationships that fucked us up. We've all been rejected, cheated on or abandoned. It's difficult as hell, I know. Those experiences leave long-lasting marks on your ability to trust people again.

More importantly, they shape your personality and make you see the world in a different way. They create a series of beliefs that condition your reality, without you even noticing. So how can you free yourself from them?

Let's dive in.

How Was Your Childhood?

Real love is not something you need to earn, nor is it something you have to fight for. It's something you deserve just because you exist.

The problem is, many of us didn't receive love in the very first stages of our life — and those stages teach us what we know about love and relationships.

Not receiving the love we needed makes us develop coping mechanisms to avoid pain and loneliness. It leads us to push people away, to sabotage ourselves and to do everything we can to never be vulnerable again.

*"As part of developing our wounded self, we unconsciously decided that who we really are — our magnificent soul essence — was not good enough. **We reasoned that if we were good enough, we would be loved. As little children, we could not understand that not being unconditionally loved had nothing to do with us.** That it was because our parents, coming from their own ego-wounded self, simply didn't know how."*

This means that, if you truly want to understand and break down your beliefs about love, you need to go within and look at your childhood.

- Were your parents present?

- As a child, did you feel loved by them — unconditionally loved?

- Did you live in a stable, caring, supportive environment?

- Or did you feel like you had to prove yourself in order to receive love? (Like getting good grades, being the golden child)

- Did your parents accept you for who you are, or were they constantly trying to change you?

Take the time to get in touch with how you feel about yourself and about your parents. **Be honest about your hidden feelings, memories, wounds and thoughts.** Don't be afraid — I know it hurts, but this is how you heal.

To make it easier for you, I'll give you my story. I was adopted when I was a baby. My parents were always honest about it and they never did anything from me, so I never thought of my adoption as something that influenced me.

However, the impact was there, and it was huge.

Unconsciously, I have always carried this **deep fear of abandonment and rejection** — because I was abandoned in the very moment I was born.

I absorbed the message that I was not good enough — if I was, why would my biological parents reject me?

Besides, my father's authoritarian parenting style only reinforced this idea. I had to follow his rules and meet his high standards, without ever having the space to express myself. He was never satisfied with anything I did.

Living with the constant burden of pleasing him made me build one more belief: that my feelings and opinions don't matter. If they did matter, why wasn't I allowed to express them? Why did I have to follow every rule without saying a word?

The 4 Types of Attachment

The attachment style you've developed, based on your relationship with your parents, will affect how you behave and interact in your romantic relationships.

Nowadays, psychologists recognize 4 main attachment styles:

- **Secure attachment:** you're comfortable with intimacy, without worrying about being rejected or abandoned. You have the ability to form secure, loving relationships with others. You're able to depend on others without becoming totally dependent.

- **Anxious attachment:** this attachment style is the one associated with neediness. You have a deep fear of abandonment, you seek constant validation and you feel that your partner doesn't care enough about you.

- **Avoidant attachment:** People with an avoidant attachment style tend to have trouble getting close to others or trusting others in relationships. You're emotionally unavailable and prefer to maintain your independence.

- **Anxious-avoidant attachment:** it's a combination of both the anxious and avoidant attachment styles. You desperately crave intimacy, yet you also avoid it at all costs. You have a need to feel loved but you're afraid of forming close bonds with others.

For many years, I lived with an anxious-avoidant attachment style. After a lot of introspection and inner work, I was able to change my attachment style to secure.

*"Attachment patterns are passed down from one generation to the next. Children learn how to connect from parents and caregivers, and they in turn teach the next generation. Your attachment history plays a crucial role in determining how you relate in adult romantic relationships, and how you relate to your children. **However, it is not what happened to you as a child that matters most — it is how you deal with it. Many people go from victim to overcome.**"*

When you develop your self-awareness, you acknowledge how your childhood affected the way you see love and relationships.

It's possible to change your attachment style. I changed mine and I went from attracting toxic push-pull relationships to be in a loving, committed relationship that makes my heart glow every day.

That's what happens when we're brave enough to go within — we take our power back instead of being a victim of our circumstances.

I don't know how your childhood was like. But I do know you deserve to be loved and cared for.

You're worthy of love — including your own. Why don't you start there?

21

CHAPTER TWO

Tips for healing a broken heart

As you cope with the loss of a relationship, these tips may help you on your journey to healing.

1. Take time to grieve

If possible, try to think of the loss of the relationship as a grieving process.

"Give yourself time. Do not try to find someone new right away. "The best thing we can do is to try to honour our emotions and not judge our emotions."

To validate your emotions, it may help you to reframe your thoughts. Instead of thinking, "I shouldn't feel so sad," Bottari recommends thinking, "I am experiencing feelings of sadness, and that's OK."

While some people take time to be alone, look inward, or see a therapist to work through the complicated emotions of a breakup, others may suppress painful feelings and jump into another relationship. "I don't recommend that. We need time to heal what's been shattered.

"We need time to look within and take inventory of what patterns we may have taken into the relationship with us that no longer work. We need to tend to our wounded hearts and take the time to allow the healing to happen with time, care, gentleness, and deeper self-understanding," she says.

2. Find a new source of joy

When you make time for self-inquiry and self-reconnection, Morgan says that this can lead to connection with what may have once brought you peace, joy, or inspiration but was put on hold during your relationship.

"We may be more open to saying 'yes' to new things, people, and experiences as a way to explore a newfound sense of freedom, even if it hurts," she says.

Morgan suggests pushing yourself to do things, even when you don't feel like it. "Chances are, even after meeting a friend for lunch, you arrive home feeling better than had you stayed home," she says.

3. Make a list of what you like about yourself

When you are feeling low about yourself, consider making a list of all the good things you did for your past partner or all the qualities they liked about you — and the qualities you like about yourself.

For example, you might write a self-love list like this:

- I made him coffee in the morning.

- I picked her up from the train station when it rained.

- I put on her favourite song when she was sad.

- I reminded him about his dad's birthday.

You may also find it helpful to write out a list of positive things you'll do in future relationships.

If you'd rather not think about relationships, Morgan O. Kate suggests searching the internet for self-affirmations that resonate with you, such as:

- I am not my mistakes.

- I am enough.

- How to heal a broken heart

- There is no wrong decision.

"Recite these when you are having negative or self-defeating thoughts," Morgan says.

4. Acknowledge thoughts about your former partner

When thoughts of your ex arise, try not to stop or block them. Instead, practice being a "witness" to these thoughts. When the thoughts come up, take a step back and acknowledge them.

"You know you are experiencing them; they are passing through your mind. You observe them. You practice observing and letting them go," she explains.

"The minute you pay attention to one and label it as something 'important,' you are no longer witnessing them. You are now judging them. Judging brings more negative emotions since your expectations were not met."

5. Express your needs to others

If you're not feeling up to meeting friends out or are having a hard time following through on commitments, try to share your feelings with others.

"Try to reconsider your needs at this time and let others know what you are dealing with," "Many people have felt the same way and will understand that you might need some time to return to your normal state."

6. Turn your attention toward others

When the pain of a breakup is too hard to bear, you may find that focusing on the needs of others can help bring feelings of wellbeing and distract you from focusing on yourself.

Consider volunteering at a local soup kitchen or animal shelter, helping a friend in need with meals or cleaning, or cutting a neighbour's grass.

7. Allow emotions to flow

You may find it helpful to talk to a trusted friend, family member, or therapist about emotions related to your breakup or ex-partner.

If you're not comfortable sharing all of your feelings, consider writing them down or meditating on them. You can also engage in another project, such as painting, that may help you release what's on your mind.

8. Find relief in exercise and movement

Exercise can reduce stress. "Use exercise as a healthy outlet to manage feelings of anxiety, sadness, lethargy, and stress.

A daily walk, bike ride, or online workout video are ways to work exercise into your daily routine when you're feeling sad or stressed about the breakup.

9. Avoid activities that remind you of your ex

If you continue to feel overwhelmed by unwanted thoughts and emotions, consider staying away from places, music, and people who remind you of your ex for a little while.

"Try to go places that make you feel safe. Surround yourself with people that care about you. Go places that you have never been. Take a day trip and explore.

10. Make meaning of the breakup

If possible, try to make meaning of the relationship ending, or accept that there's no meaning to why it ended.

"Over time, you may come to realize that the end of your relationship was ultimately in your best interest. However, it is possible that you might not be able to find any positive in the relationship ending. Both are valid conclusions. Try to have faith and keep moving forward.

CHAPTER THREE

How to Find Real, Lasting Love without Looking for It

"The privilege of a lifetime is to become who you truly are." ~Carl Jung

Often when people want a new relationship, they either look for someone to complete them or they imagine sharing their life with someone just like them. So they try to present themselves in the best possible light for their imagined future partner—either as one perfect half of a whole or as an ideal version of what they believe their future partner will want.

In my experience, finding your soul mate requires a different, far more soul-enriching approach. Here are six steps that worked for me:

1. Stop looking for your soul mate and find the missing parts of you.

This may sound counterintuitive, but it's exactly how I met my husband. I stopped looking for "the one" after a two-year relationship ended, which I had believed was the one. I decided to turn my attention inward—to get to know and accept myself, to heal past wounds, and to explore and develop new parts of myself.

Previously, I needed to be with someone in order to feel content, to have someone love me in order to feel loved. Breaking up with past boyfriends was so painful because it felt as if *I* was breaking up, as if I was being torn from a part of *myself*.

What I discovered was that I had to learn to be whole. And when I started to work on that, my life changed.

2. Live your life as you want to live it.

When I started to discover more about myself and to follow my own path, I started to live a life that was meaningful to *me*. I was no longer following someone else's rules and ideas about what I should do.

This can disappoint some people close to you, such as your family. But if you want to find fulfilment in your life, you have to fulfil yourself, not someone else!

And doing what is right for you means you will be in places, jobs, and near people that are aligned with your life path, and with *you*. So you will have a much better chance of meeting your soul mate, because your soul mate will also be connected to your life path.

3. Stop trying to appeal to an imagined, potential partner.

A side effect of leading the life you choose is that you automatically become more attractive. You become more real, authentic, substantial, valuable, passionate, happy, and present. This makes you more beautiful in a natural and effortless way, and it will also make you attractive to your soul mate.

Whereas when you *try* to make yourself attractive in order to find someone, you alter the way you behave and present yourself so that if your soul mate were to show up, he or she might not even recognize you.

So just be yourself, whether that means you dress in corporate attire or resort wear, or casual clothing or more formal, or if your preference changes at different times.

You don't need to be a particular weight or have large biceps or wear uncomfortable shoes if you don't like them. Go to the gym only if you love it, do yoga if you love it, walk or surf or cycle if you enjoy those activities.

A partner who you will be with over the long term will not make a decision about your worth based on a superficial aspect of your appearance. So tap into what feels right for you, do the activities you enjoy, wear the clothes that suit you and in which you feel comfortable.

You will be far more attractive to your soul mate if you look like *yourself* when you meet them.

4. If you are attracted to particular qualities in someone else, find or develop those qualities in yourself.

Most of us express only a small part of who we are. We limit ourselves to the personality—or self—we have become in response to our childhood environment. This is an unavoidable stage in our developmental process because we have to form a self—or ego—that enables us to survive and hopefully thrive in our family and social setting.

And the way we do that is by developing characteristics that meet our survival needs and pushing away any characteristics that aren't valued or needed.

So we all have hidden or disowned parts of ourselves that at some point we need to unearth.

When we haven't yet unearthed and embraced our disowned parts, we are drawn into relationships with others who express those parts. It is like we are unconsciously trying to complete ourselves through our relationships.

These relationships usually involve intense attraction at first and are characterized by feelings of completeness. But inevitably, they become stifled by strong relationship patterns that form where people get stuck relating to one another from one main part of themselves that bonds with its opposite in the other person. These are called "bonding patterns."

So, for example, a very responsible man might become a "responsible father" in relation to his partner's inner "pleasing daughter," and a nurturing woman might become a "nurturing mother" to her partner's inner "needy son."

If the woman doesn't become conscious of her own responsibility, she will rely on her partner to be responsible. And if the man doesn't connect with his nurturing side, he will want to be nurtured by her. But then when stresses and vulnerabilities arise in the relationship, these bonding patterns turn negative, and the partners turn on each other.

I am so grateful to have learned about bonding patterns because the awareness of them not only helps enormously in my relationship, but they also act as a guide for which parts of myself I have lost connection to.

Because bonding patterns are the natural way that we give and receive love, they are unavoidable. And no matter how conscious we become, there is always something that's unconscious! But bonding patterns *can* be navigated successfully.

When you become aware that you are attracted to other people because of what you have disowned in yourself, and then work on owning those qualities in yourself, your relationships transform.

If you are in a relationship already and you begin this process, then as you and your partner reclaim your disowned selves, you start to become more fully yourselves with each other and your relationship will become richer.

5. Engage with life; accept the gifts that are offered to you.

The night I met my husband a friend had invited me to a party hosted by one of her friends, and at first I wasn't sure if I wanted to go.

I was tempted to decline the invitation because I didn't know the person whose party it was, and it was a Sunday night, so I had work the next day. But I didn't have a compelling reason not to go and I had promised myself that I would accept the gifts life offered me, such as saying yes to invitations that seemed to come from nowhere. And this was one of those.

When I got to that party, there he was: my future husband, with whom I have had three children and twenty-five years of a wonderful life together.

Was I looking for someone when I went to that party?

No. And it was a surprise to meet him there. If I had been intentionally looking for a partner, I probably would not have even spoken to my husband that night.

When you look at each person you encounter as if you are screening them for a job with a life-long contract, it changes the organic flow of events and natural connection that forms with the people you encounter. It is also off-putting to be evaluated as a "catch" and it is likely to make people run from you!

The simplest way to stop assessing others as potential life partners is to just stop looking for a partner and connect with the people you meet with genuine interest. Then enjoy the type of relationship that naturally develops—or doesn't—whether that's a friendship, a business connection, or a bond based on a mutual interest.

6. When you meet someone, don't hurry things; allow the relationship to unfold.

When you meet someone you have a good connection with, allow that connection to develop and grow. If the person is a soul mate, he or she will also be into you, so if you both pay genuine attention to each other then something will develop.

There is no need to play games or to try particular seduction techniques or to achieve milestones by a particular time. A successful long-term relationship is not a game.

Do you really want to be in a relationship with someone you had to manipulate into it? Do you want your partner to be enchanted by an image you have created so that you have to hide yourself in some way? Or do you want your partner to love you wholeheartedly? What kind of relationship do you want to bring children into if you end up having them?

Each relationship is unique, just as each person is unique, so how your relationship unfolds will be unique too. You can't plan for it to go a particular way. You have to engage with the process of it and with each other, and then make decisions as you go. There is no one line you can say, no one action you can take, that will lead to a particular result.

All you can do is live your life more fully, learn to accept and love yourself more fully, and you will love and be loved more fully.

The Importance of Healing After a Breakup

There is beauty in the struggle of loving ourselves more.

CHAPTER FOUR

The Importance of Healing After a Breakup

There is beauty in the struggle of loving ourselves more.

Healing after a breakup can be quite a dark journey, but it's an essential part of our growth and having a more fruitful relationship in the foreseeable future. For many people like myself, I never saw the beauty in healing. I thought the power was in moving on instantly and being open to dating right after coming out of a relationship/situationship. I used to be a serial dater and played victim like it was nobody's business.

About two years ago, my toxic way of thinking used to be, yeah, it was his fault we didn't work out–he just chose to leave me like the rest of them. It wasn't until my last relationship that I realized I was just playing the blame game and not being accountable for my end of the partnership.

I felt like I always had a void to fill, and I knew being alone for some time wasn't exactly the option I thought I needed to do – and I avoided doing it. I went through the phase of overusing dating apps, and noticed I was beginning to see men as just a disposable swipe, just a face, not too concerned about character and values. My solution became I dated someone new to get over someone else and hoped to find my partner for life along the way.

Thinking back on how I used to think made me feel a bit shameful initially, but as time went on, I thought of it as this was what I knew then, and that season also serves a purpose for shaping the woman I am today. In order to change my perspective, I had to take a 360-approach to any triggers and hold myself accountable for doing better. You can't do the same thing expecting better results – that's just insanity.

What should you NOT do after a breakup?

Do not go rushing back to your ex for closure. There is a reason you guys broke up, whether it be for good or maybe you guys are able to get back together after working on each other's issues separately. But right now, we don't know where the future will take either of you, so you have to only focus on you! Create our own closure, and it shouldn't start with hate but appreciation of what you learned from that relationship.

Leave the dating apps alone for now or forever.

The unfortunate truth is that most people don't like being alone; they quickly feel lonely and go to others to fill that void. You will never be a whole, healthy partner until you make it entirely your responsibility to be happy. Don't go running to friends with benefits or dating in general either because that's just another layer of avoidance to not deal with your reality. This is a season of discipline, and in order for you to learn the lesson, you have to hold yourself to high standards to attain a healthy and healed mind-set.

CHAPTER FIVE

What are the stages of healing after a breakup?

Allow yourself to grieve and mourn your significant other. You are allowed to cry; despite what others say, it's not a sign of weakness; it's just a human trait we all have expressing deep emotions. It doesn't mean you aren't going to deal with your healing process; you are doing that now, and as time progresses, those tears will come to an end.

Therapy is a great adventure to explore after a relationship. It will help analyse your feelings in the partnership and point out areas you fell short in because that's all you have control of – is yourself. They will ask questions regarding if you paid attention to red flags and did you address them? Did you feel like you settled for less? Were you vocal about things you were uncomfortable with, or did you keep enabling traits you weren't fond of? What was your argument style like? Etc.

Signs you're healing from the breakup

Remember the date you set for being single? Well, you threw it out the window because you are finding contentment and joy in your solitude! You'll know your healing when the waterworks come to an end or just occur less. You're able to look at the relationship for all that it helped you grow as a person, and you're hoping for the absolute best for your ex-partner.

The best part of it all is that you're finally seeing your whole worth! Your worth isn't defined by partnership; your worth is determined by how much you know and value yourself and hold others accountable for meeting those standards. You will be handing out a lot of rejection letters once you know your value because most people don't deserve access to you.

Healing is not Destination: it's a journey. So have grace with this process and get used to loving yourself more; no one can fill your love cup up like you!

CHAPTER SIX

Steps for How to Move On:

Look at your life as a journey

It's important to keep in mind that everyone who's doing okay now has had moments when they thought they'd never be okay. A breakup may feel like the end of the world, but years from now, a struggle of today will feel like a lesson from the past. The more we can look at our lives as fluid and not fixed, the more we can see our experiences in perspective. The end of a relationship is not the end of our story. Whether we're with someone or on our own, no one else can possess our story or our identity. We may leave a relationship feeling like we left part of ourselves behind, wondering how to move on without the other person, but the truth is we are still whole, still evolving, and still growing all the time.

Keeping the imagery of movement in our minds is a way of preventing ourselves from being caught in the whirlpool of an inner critic that tells us we will never be able to move on or feel like ourselves again.

Silence your inner critic

The "critical inner voice" is a term used to describe a negative thought process we all have that is like an internalized nemesis. This cruel "voice" criticizes, coaches, and even pities us (and others) in ways that undermine us when we're up and kick us when we're down. A lot of the pain and suffering we experience after a breakup is owed to this inner critic. Common post-breakup "voices" include:

- "I told you she would leave you."

- "You have nothing now."

- "No one will ever love you."

- "You'll always be alone."

- "You can't trust people."

- "You should just forget about relationships."

- "Have a drink. It will make you feel better."

- "Just be alone. No one wants to see you right now."

Getting caught up in this internal dialogue makes the process of figuring out how to move on much more difficult.

Reflect realistically

There is always real loss that comes with breaking up, however, we also tend to look back on our relationships with a zoom lens on the good and blinders on the bad. "Reflect on the relationship for what it was," advised Dr. Karen Weinstein in an interview with Business Insider. "Resist the common tendency to idealize the relationship. It's very common to only recall and focus on the wonderful aspects of the relationship. This makes it even harder to accept the reality that it's over and is the equivalent of 'denial' in the stages of grief." Remembering that there were struggles and issues in the relationship and real reasons why we are no longer together can help us feel more resilient and resolved toward moving on.

Let go of fantasy

Idealizing our partner or a relationship isn't just something that happens after we split up. Often, couples enter into what Dr. Firestone calls a "fantasy bond," an illusion of connection that replaces real relating and genuine acts of love and intimacy. Symptoms of a fantasy bond can include relating as a unit, valuing the form of being a couple over the substance of making contact, falling into routine, lacking independence, engaging in less affection, and entering into dynamics of control and submission as opposed to equality. The quality of the relationship often deteriorates as real love is replaced with a fantasy bond. The couple may stay together based on a fantasy that their partner will somehow "save" them. Or, they may split up, because the elements that first drew them together are no longer operating.

When we're in a fantasy bond and the relationship ends, it's even harder to move on, because we don't only mourn the loss of the person but the loss of the fantasy. This fantasy dynamic can also lead us to continue to look at the person we lost through an idealized lens. "When a fantasy bond is broken, we are more likely to mourn the end of our false sense of security than the end of real, loving relating," wrote Dr. Lisa Firestone. "When we break up with someone, and we are willing to let go of this illusion of connection, we might find that we are far less devastated by the separation." Breaking the fantasy bond with a former partner is often key to moving on.

Feel the feelings

It's normal to be emotionally raw after a breakup. Although, these feelings can feel overwhelming, we should remember that emotion comes in waves. It arrives, peaks, and subsides. Accepting our feelings is part of the path to healing. Treat yourself the way you would a friend, and give yourself a break. We can acknowledge the sadness, anger, or fear that arises without handing these feelings over to our inner critic. Remember that our feelings are acceptable, but the thoughts around the feelings, like "you'll never find anyone else" or "you can't live without him or her" are not.

Talk about it

Some people believe the way to move on is to just shut down and not talk about it. According to HelpGuide.org, this is the opposite approach to take. "Even if it is difficult for you to talk about your feelings with other people, it is very important to find a way to do so when you are grieving. Knowing that others are aware of your feelings will make you feel less alone with your pain and will help you heal." Sharing our experience with someone who's been through it, someone who we trust and can offer sympathy, or someone who helps put us in a good mood is a smart (and unselfish) idea. People want to be there for one another. We may also benefit from seeking the help of a therapist and having a safe and specific outlet for what we're going through emotionally.

Explore your attachment style

A recent study at Pace University showed that how people respond to breakups has a lot to do with their attachment style. The study found that "individuals who reported higher self-esteem, less rejection sensitivity, and lower levels of attachment anxiety reported less adverse effects to break-up." Learning about how our attachment style impacts our relationships may help us make sense of our own, intense reactions to splitting up. It can also guide us to understand how we operate and why we feel the ways we do in our relationships, in general. For example, perhaps we felt more insecure and clingy toward our partner based on early attachment patterns. Understanding our attachment history can also orient us toward forming more secure attachments in future relationships.

Believe in yourself

Stanford researchers recently discovered that a person's "basic beliefs about personality can contribute to whether [they] recover from, or remain mired in, the pain of rejection." They found that individuals who saw personality as fixed were more likely to blame themselves and their "toxic personalities" for the breakup. They were more likely to question and criticize themselves and feel more hopeless about their romantic future. However, individuals who saw their personalities as "changeable" were more inclined to view their breakup as an opportunity to grow, develop, and change. They were hopeful about their future relationships and were able to move on more easily. If we can stand up to our inner critic and believe in our own adaptability, we can actually figure out how to move on more successfully.

Embrace self-compassion

Self-compassion can be a key ingredient to healing from a breakup. "If you pick all of the variables that predict how people will do after their marriage ends, self-compassion really carries the day," said researcher David Sbarra of University of Arizona, after interviewing more than 100 recently divorced individuals. According to Greater Good Magazine, Sbarra's research showed that "those with high self-compassion reported fewer intrusive negative thoughts, fewer bad dreams about the divorce, and less negative rumination. Self-compassion had a greater impact than other traits, habits, or even practical details."

Dr. Kristin Neff, a lead researcher on self-compassion wrote that it "involves acting the same way towards yourself when you are having a difficult time, fail, or notice something you don't like about yourself. Instead of just ignoring your pain with a 'stiff upper lip' mentality, you stop to tell yourself 'this is really difficult right now,' how can I comfort and care for myself in this moment?" She defines self-compassion as having three main elements:

1. Self-kindness as opposed to self-judgment
2. Common humanity as opposed to isolation
3. Mindfulness as opposed to over-identification

Embracing each of these elements can help us on our journey as we discover how to move on.

Practicing mindfulness

Dr. Lisa Firestone describes mindfulness as "an incredible tool to help people understand, tolerate, and deal with their emotions in healthy ways." Practicing mindfulness meditation has been shown to reduce stress by teaching us to accept our thoughts and feelings without over-identifying and being overwhelmed by them or judging ourselves harshly.

Headspace is an app that guides people through simple mindfulness exercises, allowing them to easily integrate a practice into daily life. Their suggestions for using mindfulness to get through a breakup include paying attention to the stories our mind is telling us, acknowledging them, but not necessarily believing them, letting ourselves feel our emotions, focusing on gratitude, and making time each day for a mindfulness exercise. "Sitting mindfully with intense emotions may seem like the last thing you want to do," they write. "But it is a critical step in the healing process."

Don't ruminate

One of the main benefits of mindfulness is that it helps us to avoid rumination. A recent UK study of more than 30,000 people showed that harping on negative life events (particularly through rumination and self-blame) can be the prime predictor of some of the most common mental health problems. So, while we should certainly talk openly about our struggles and feel our feelings about a breakup, we should be wary of indulging in obsessive or sinking thoughts that lead us down a dark path. We can help ourselves catch on to when we start ruminating when we notice our critical inner voices creeping in or our mood shifting for the worse.

Find a support team

Our friends can be the best tool we have when we're figuring out how to move on. Whenever we are experiencing any difficulty or transition in life, it's helpful to put together a support team, a group of people we know we can turn to when we feel our worst. This list can be long or short. It can include family, friends, counsellors, or co-workers. The only criteria is that we choose people who help us feel positive and more like ourselves. Seeking the company of someone who tends to ruminate or commiserate with us isn't the most effective way to help ourselves move on. Our support team should include people with whom we can be open, honest, and emotive, but who also make sure to help us steer our thoughts away from our inner critic.

Practice self-care

When we're stuck in the pain and confusion of a breakup, we often forget to take care of ourselves. Losing sleep or sleeping too much, eating too much or too little, drinking alcohol, or engaging in less activity can exacerbate negative emotions. No matter how low we feel, we should treat ourselves (and our bodies) like a friend and remember to take care of them. We must remember the basics: exercise, sleep, and eat. Even light exercise or just getting outside can boost our mood by releasing endorphins. Lack of rest can make us feel more stressed, anxious, and disoriented. Too much sleep can leave us groggy or lethargic. To be of sound mind, we should strive for a balance and give ourselves the time we need to rest.

The same goes for how we eat. Whether we indulge in a box of cupcakes or start skipping meals, we are doing our minds and bodies a disservice if we aren't treating ourselves kindly. We should try eating wholesome foods that nourish our body and that we enjoy. And while it can be tempting to drink alcohol or seek the escape of a high, the lows we experience either during or following the use of a substance can be exaggerated and set us back emotionally.

Try new things and old ones, too

Deepak Chopra said, "In the process of letting go you will lose many things from the past, but you will find yourself." One of the healthiest ways to move on is to find ways to connect to yourself as an individual. If many things we like to do feel tied to our partner, we should seek out new activities and make new memories that are our own. We can try taking a class, visiting a new city, volunteering, going out with a new friend, taking up a hobby, or eating at different restaurants – anything that feels exploratory and unique to us.

On the flip side, we can also do things we used to like to do. Perhaps, there's an activity we stopped doing as much when we got into a relationship that we can try again – maybe a sport or a creative pursuit. Contrary to popular belief, we do not have to give up friends, activities, or sections of an entire city when we break up with someone. However, if certain things trigger us emotionally that we'd rather take some time away from, that's fine, too. The main objective is to do the things that make us feel the most ourselves, whether that means discovering new aspects of who we are or reconnecting with old ones.

Practice generosity

When we are suffering, we can get lost in our own worlds and minds. The more we can connect with others, the more we can forget about (or at least stop catastrophizing) our own struggles. Being generous has surprisingly healing benefits. Volunteering can be a welcome distraction and valuable use of our time. Even simply practicing small acts of generosity in a given day can help us to move on. Smiling at the person who serves us coffee, initiating a warm conversation with someone at work, making time to ask friends about what's going on in their lives, helping someone who's lost on a street corner – these are all little, positive ways to take us out of our heads, make us feel good about ourselves, and improve our outlook on the world around us.

www.ingramcontent.com/pod-product-compliance
Lightning Source LLC
Chambersburg PA
CBHW051454150726
48000CB00005B/2385